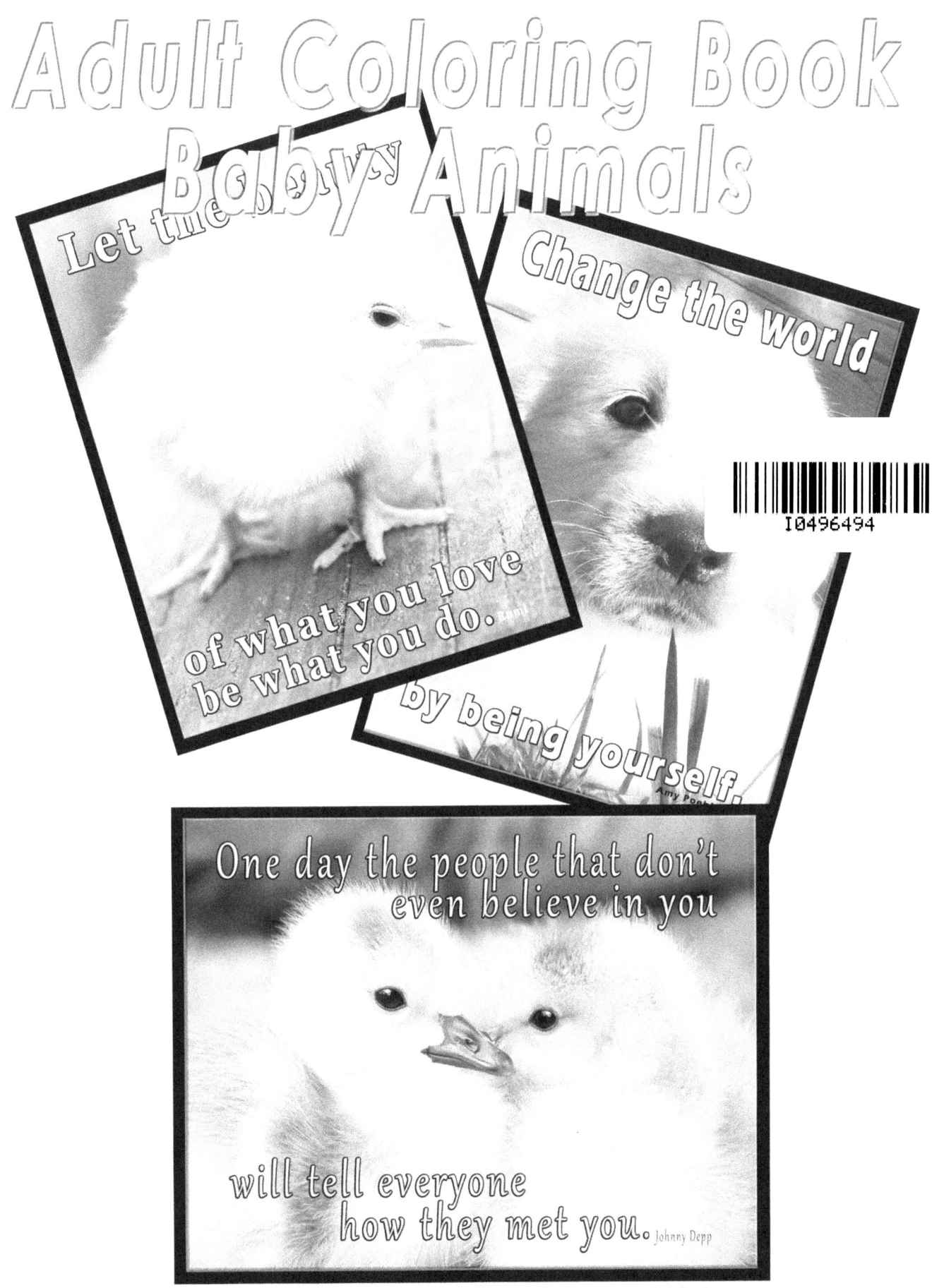

Simplicity

is the ultimate sophistication.

Leonardo da Vinci

The meaning of life is to give life meaning. — Ken Hudgins

Every moment is a fresh beginning
T.S Eliot

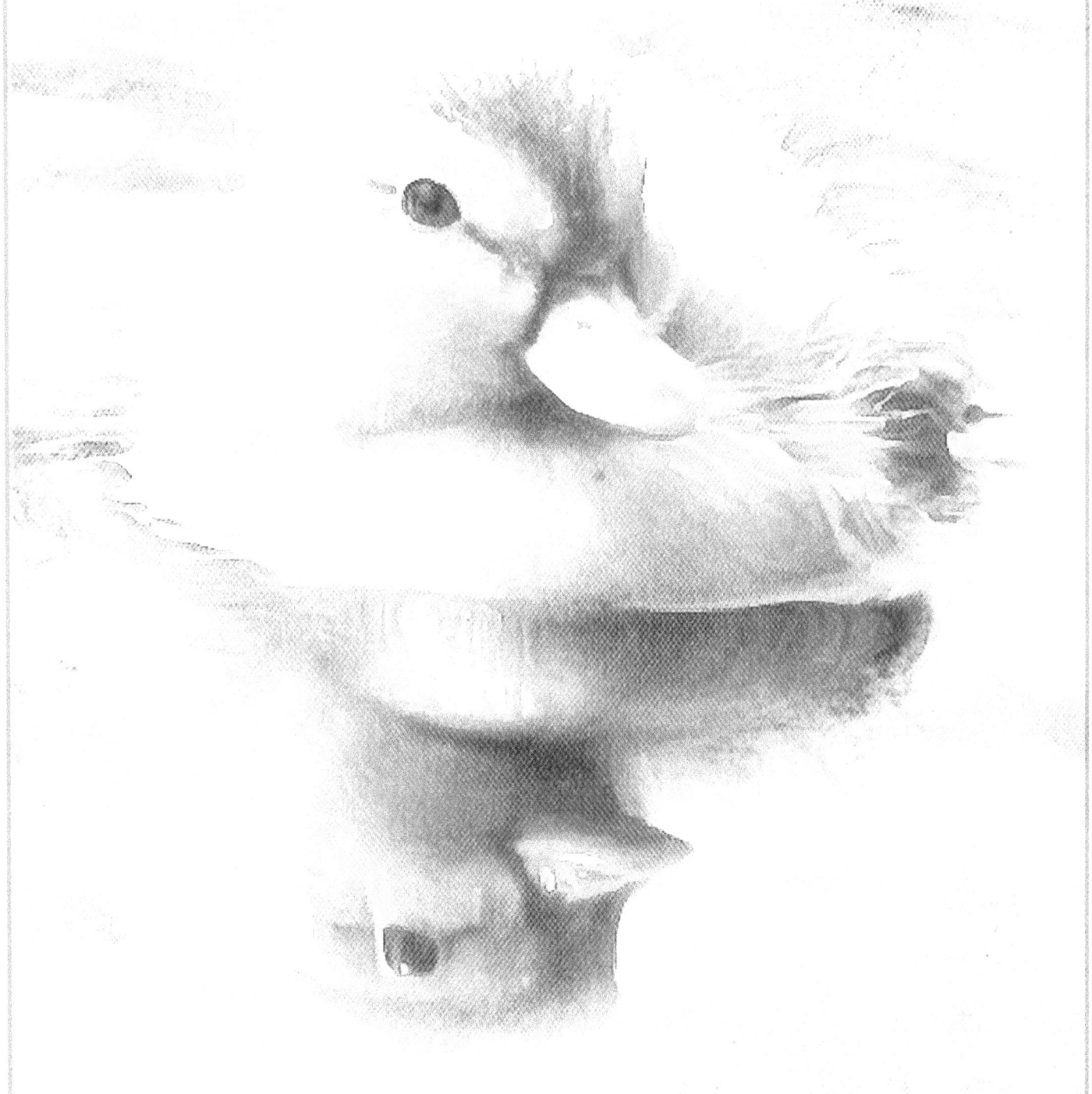

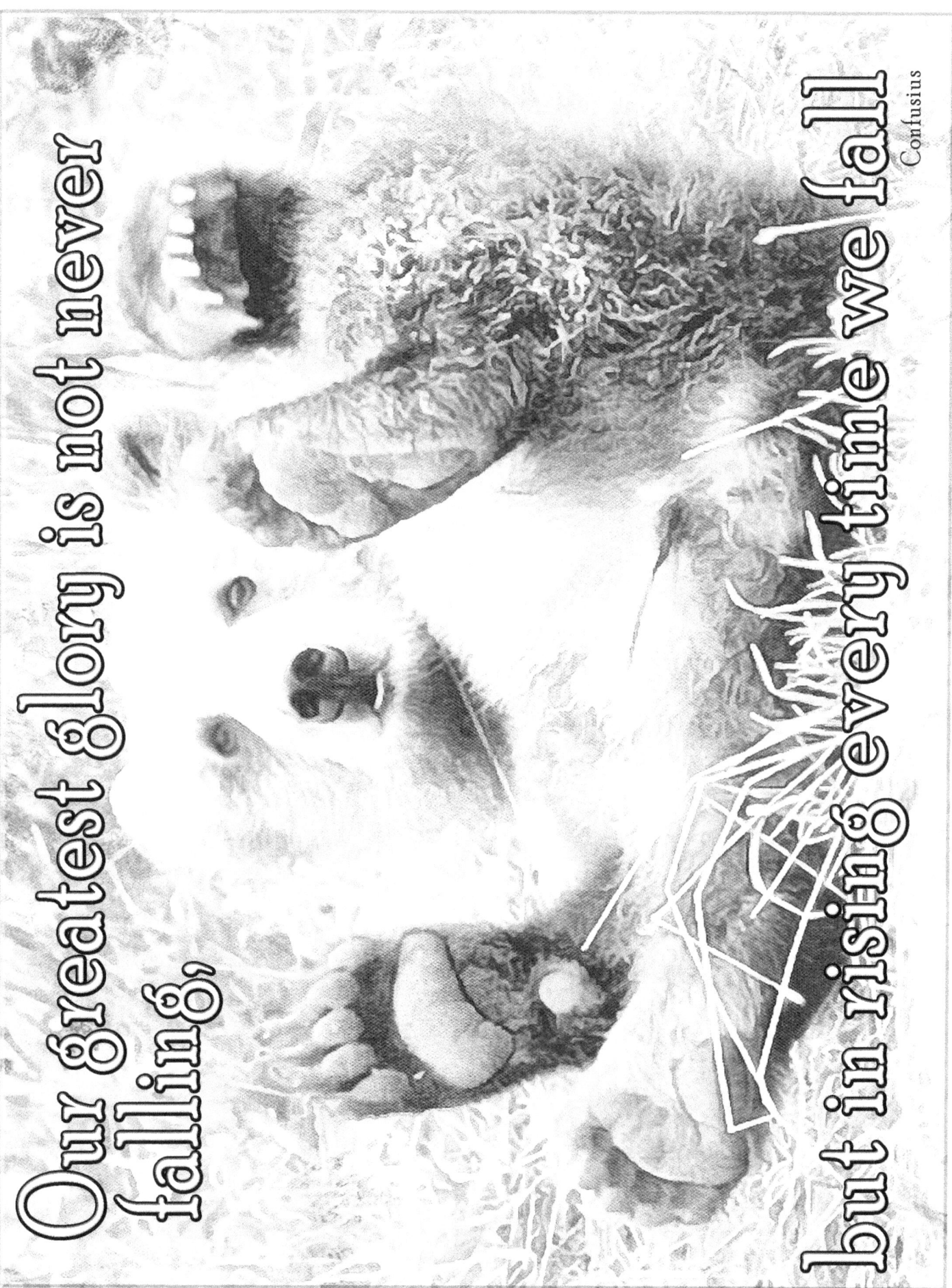

Change the world by being yourself.
Amy Poehler

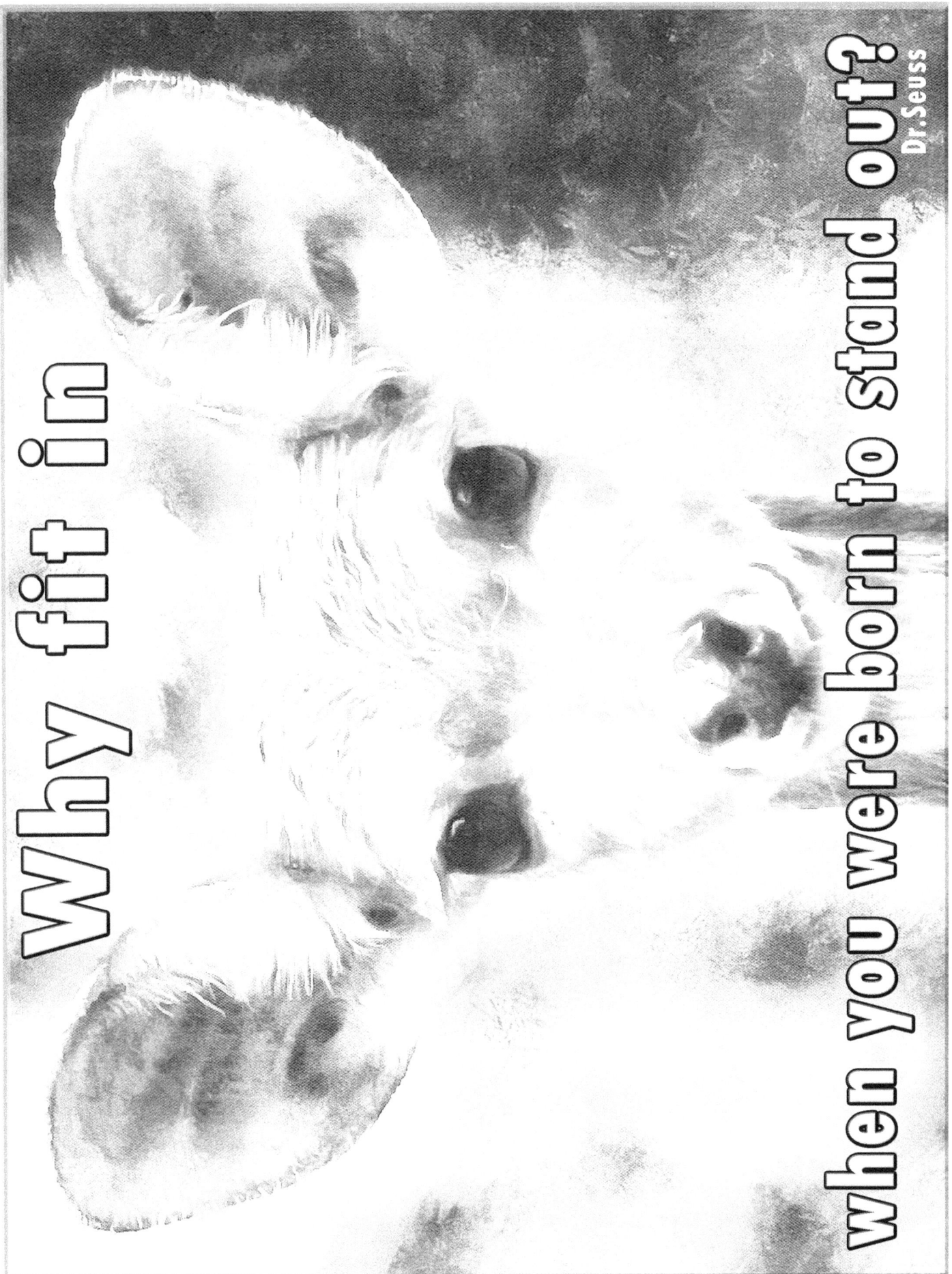

Embrace

the glorious mess that you are.
Elizabeth Gilbert

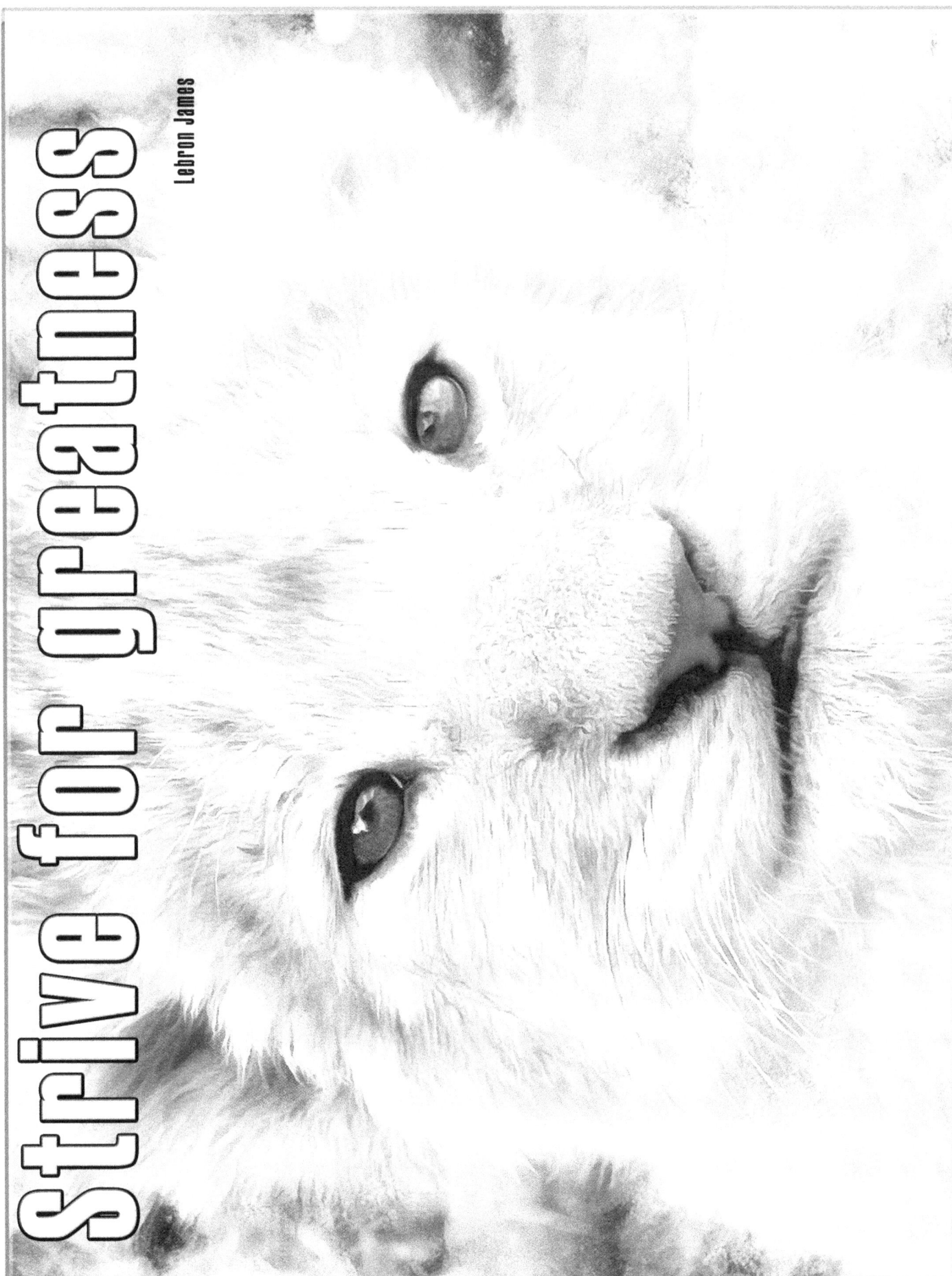

Let the beauty

of what you love be what you do. Rumi

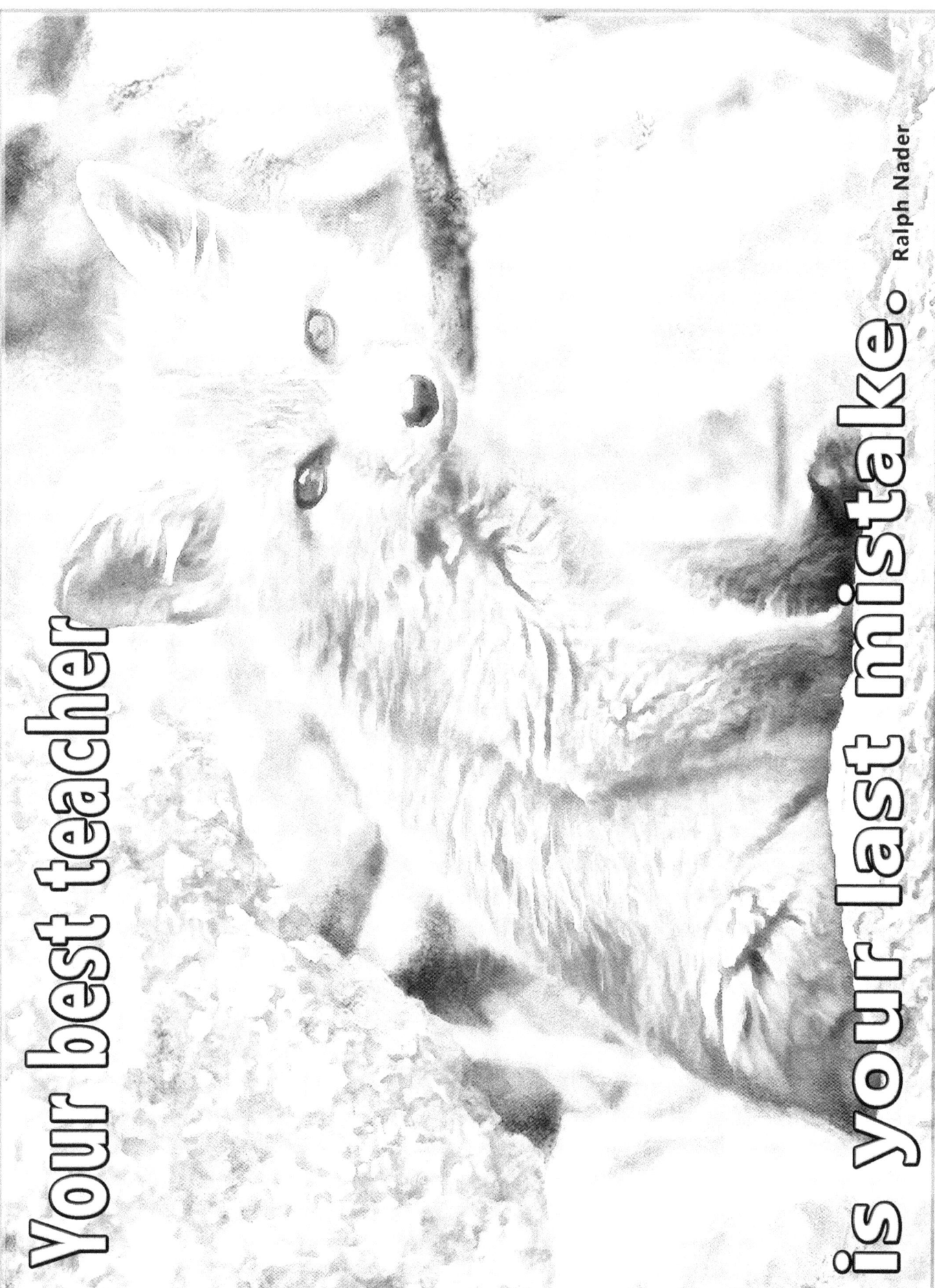

Don't you know your imperfection is a blessing?

Kendrick Lamar

To live will be an awfully big adventure. peter pan

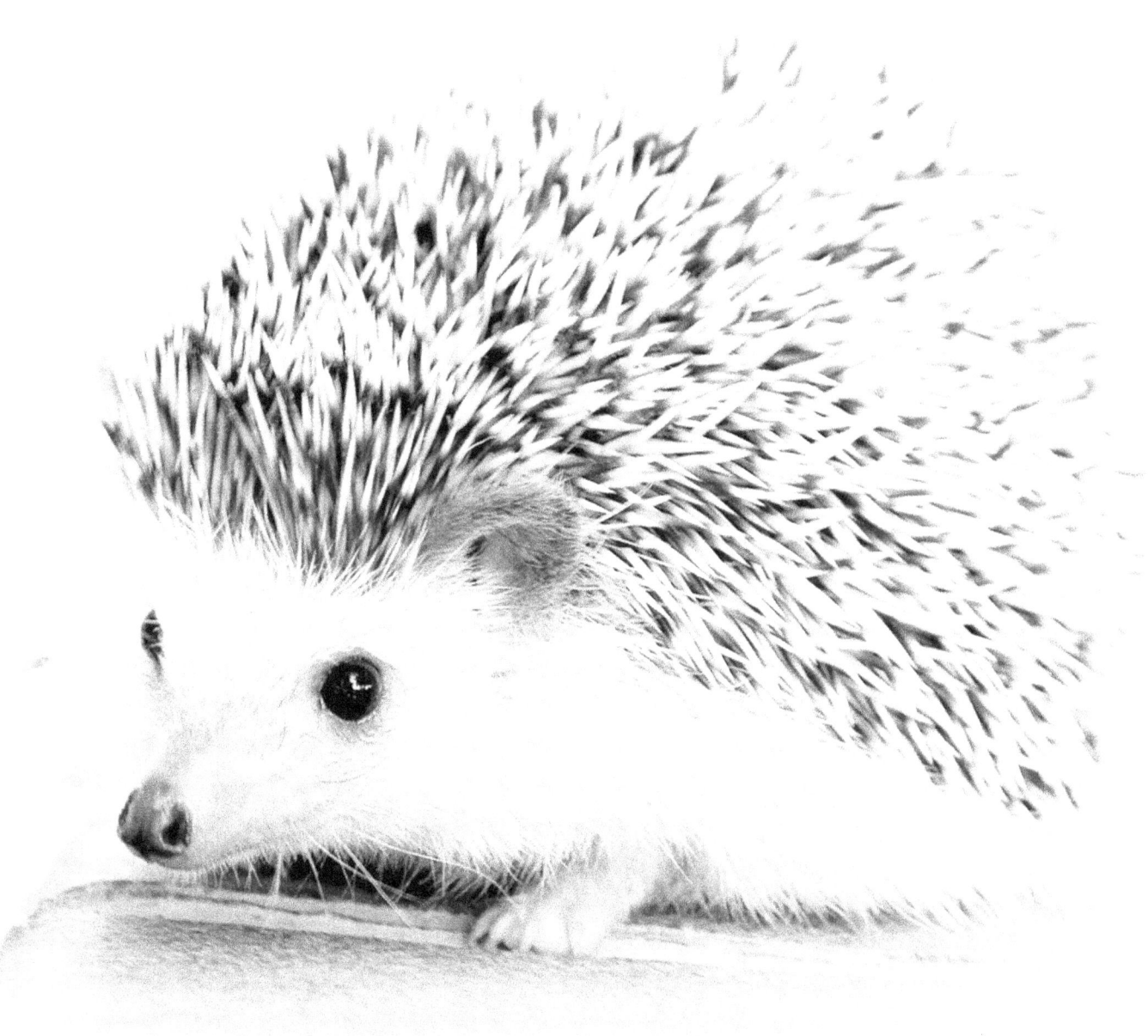

If you tell the truth you don't have to remember anything.
— Mark Twain

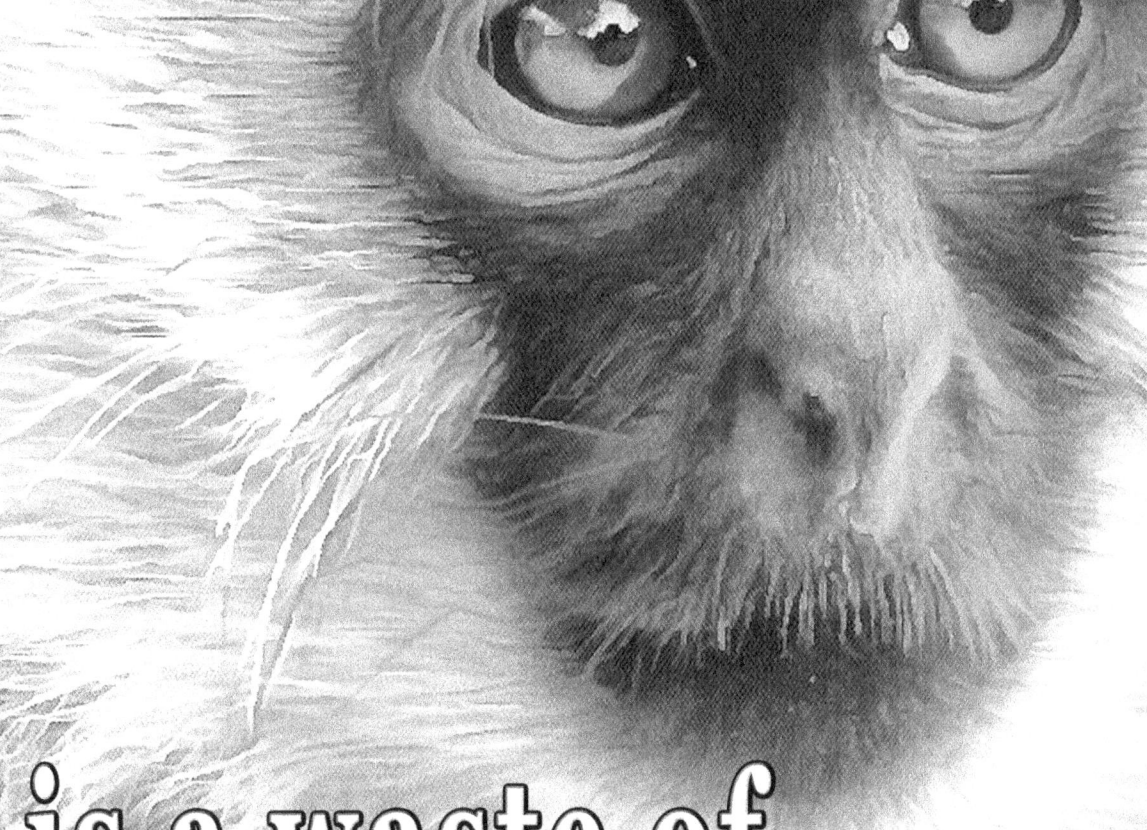

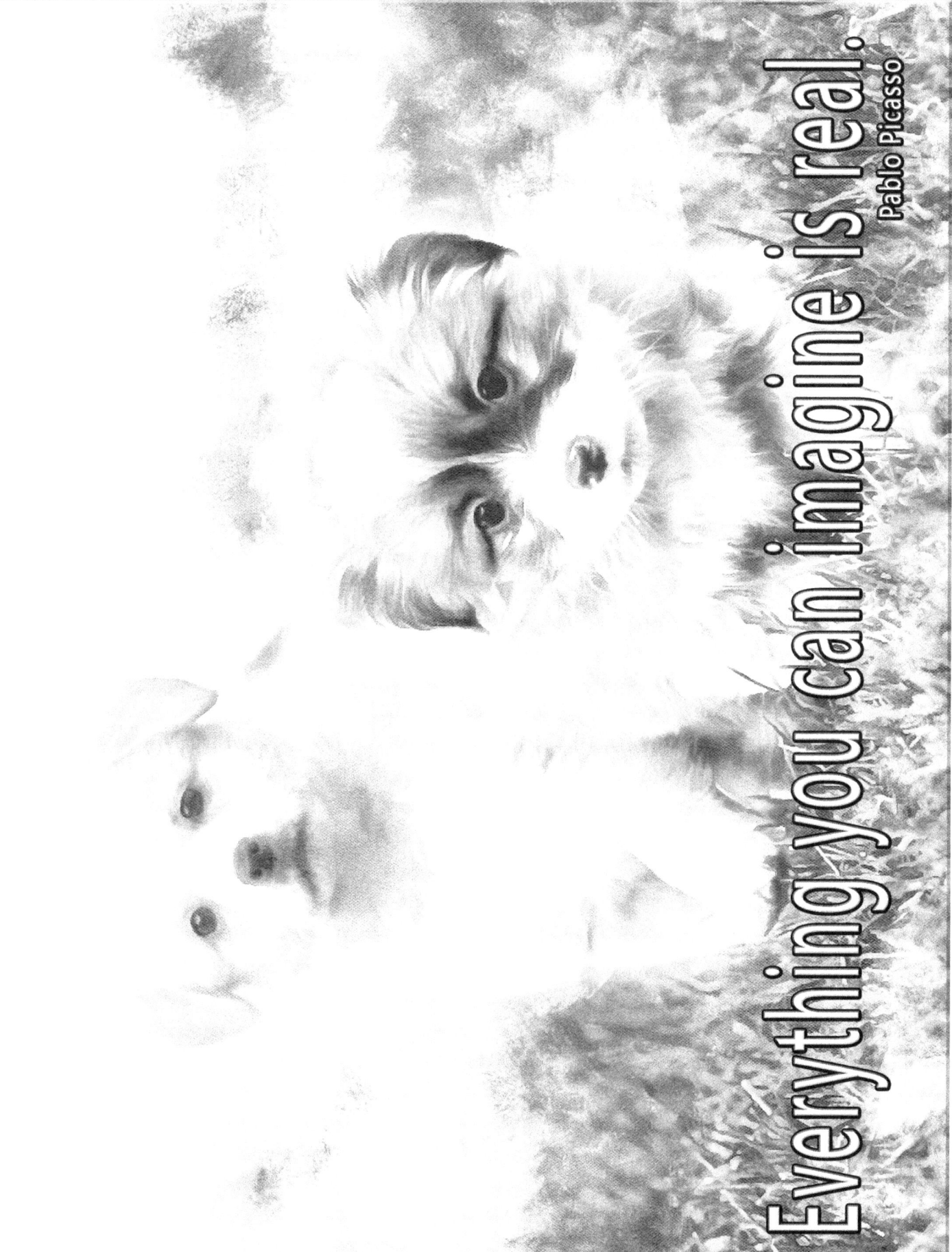

Be so good

they can't ignore you.
— Steve Martin

"The time is always right to do what is right."

— Martin Luther King Jr.

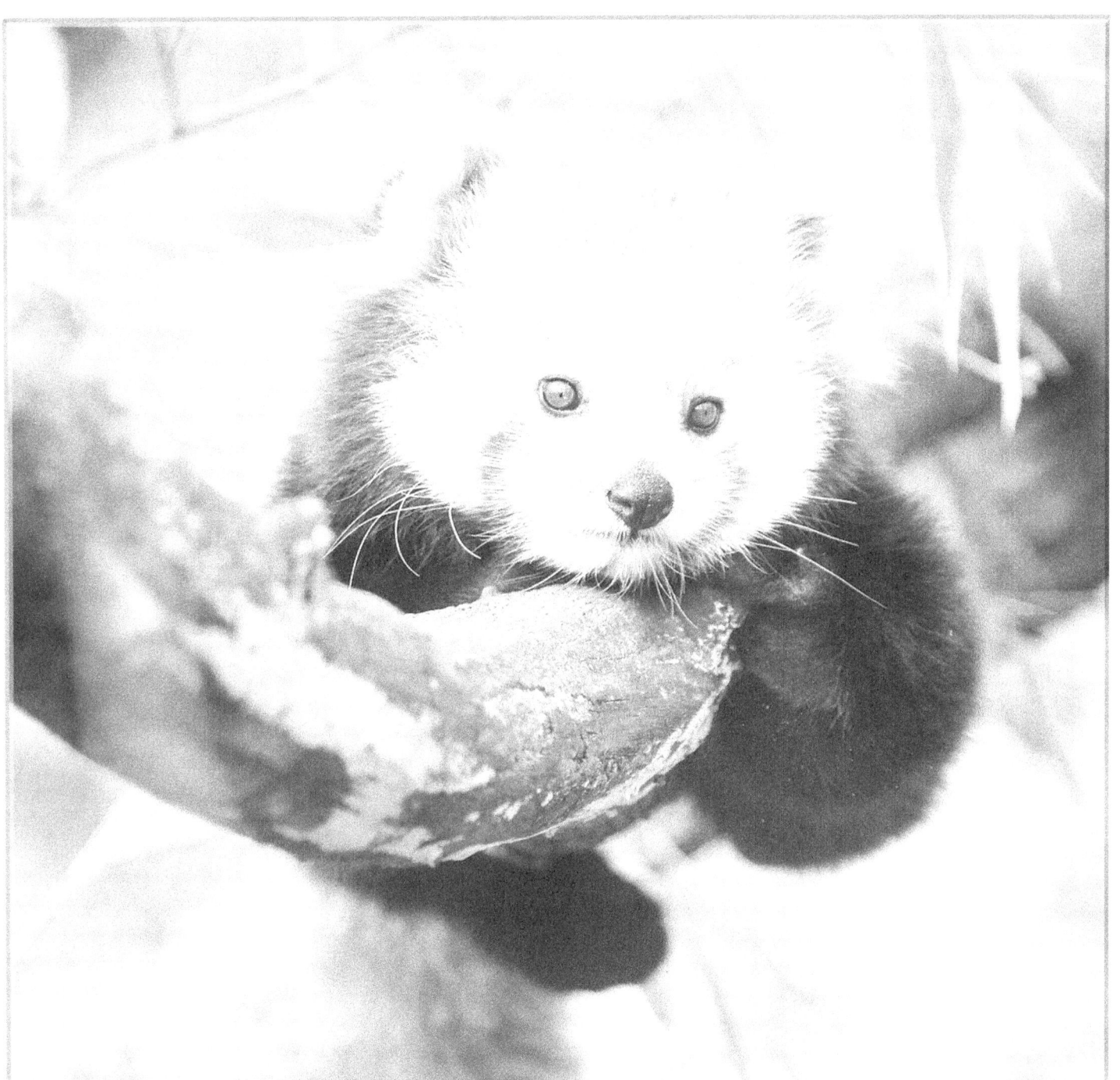

One day the people that don't even believe in you will tell everyone how they met you. — Johnny Depp

Happiness depends upon ourselves.
Aristotle

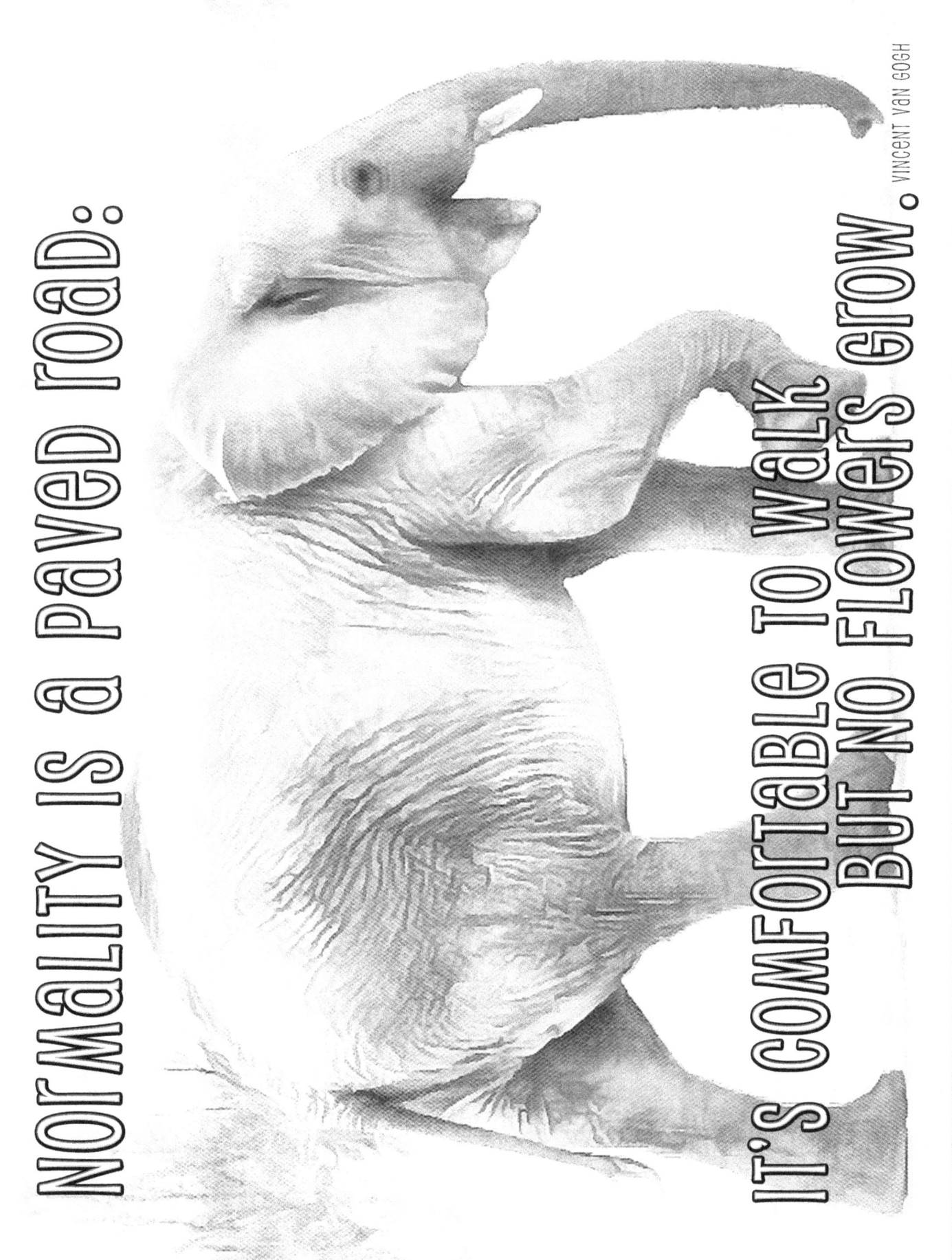

All limits

are self imposed.

Icarus

Be happy for this moment. This moment is your life. — Omar Khayyam

> What we think, we become.
> — Buddha

"I don't need it to be easy, I need it to be worth it."

— Lil Wayne

Where there is love there is life.
Mahatma Gandhi

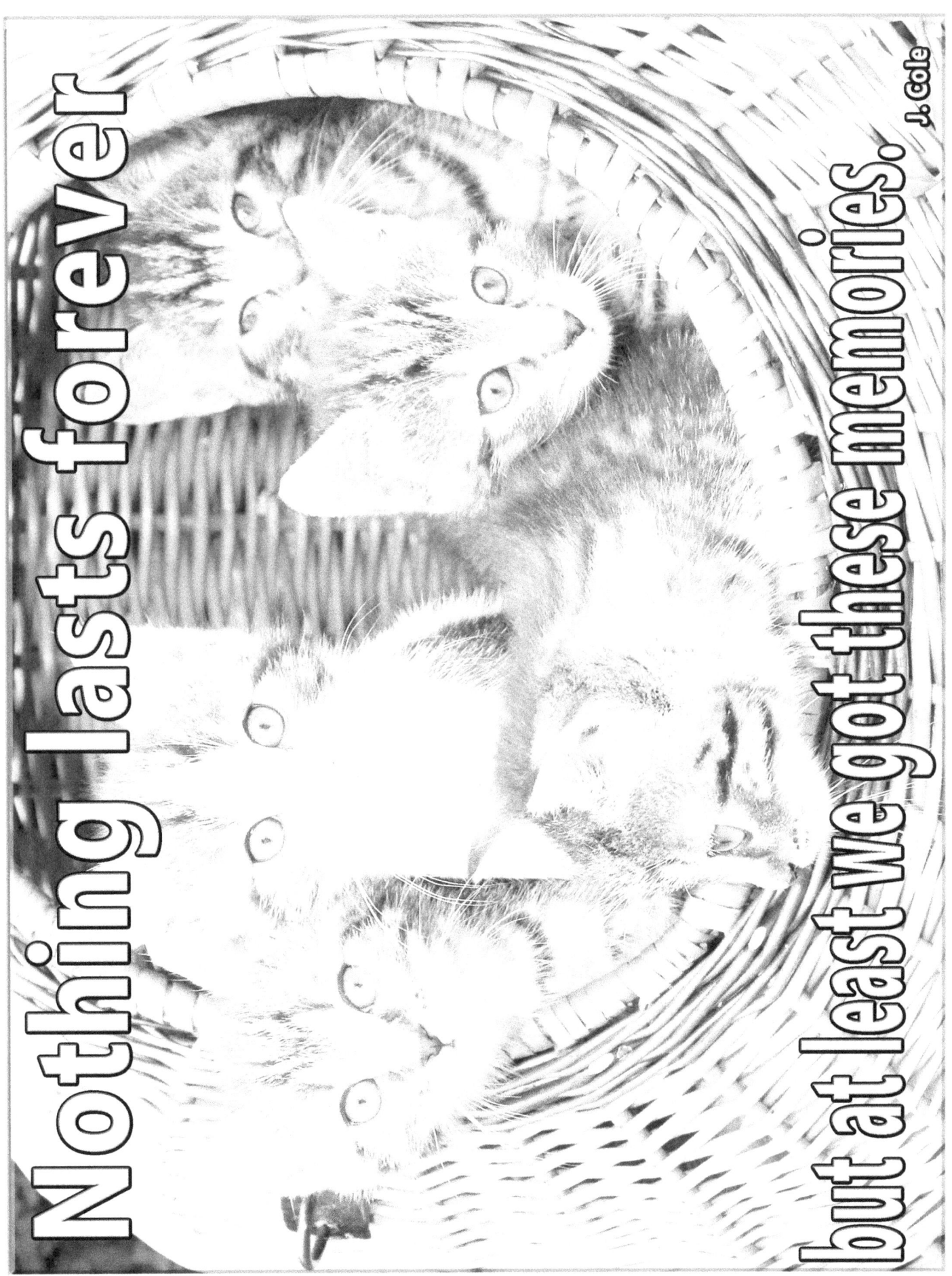

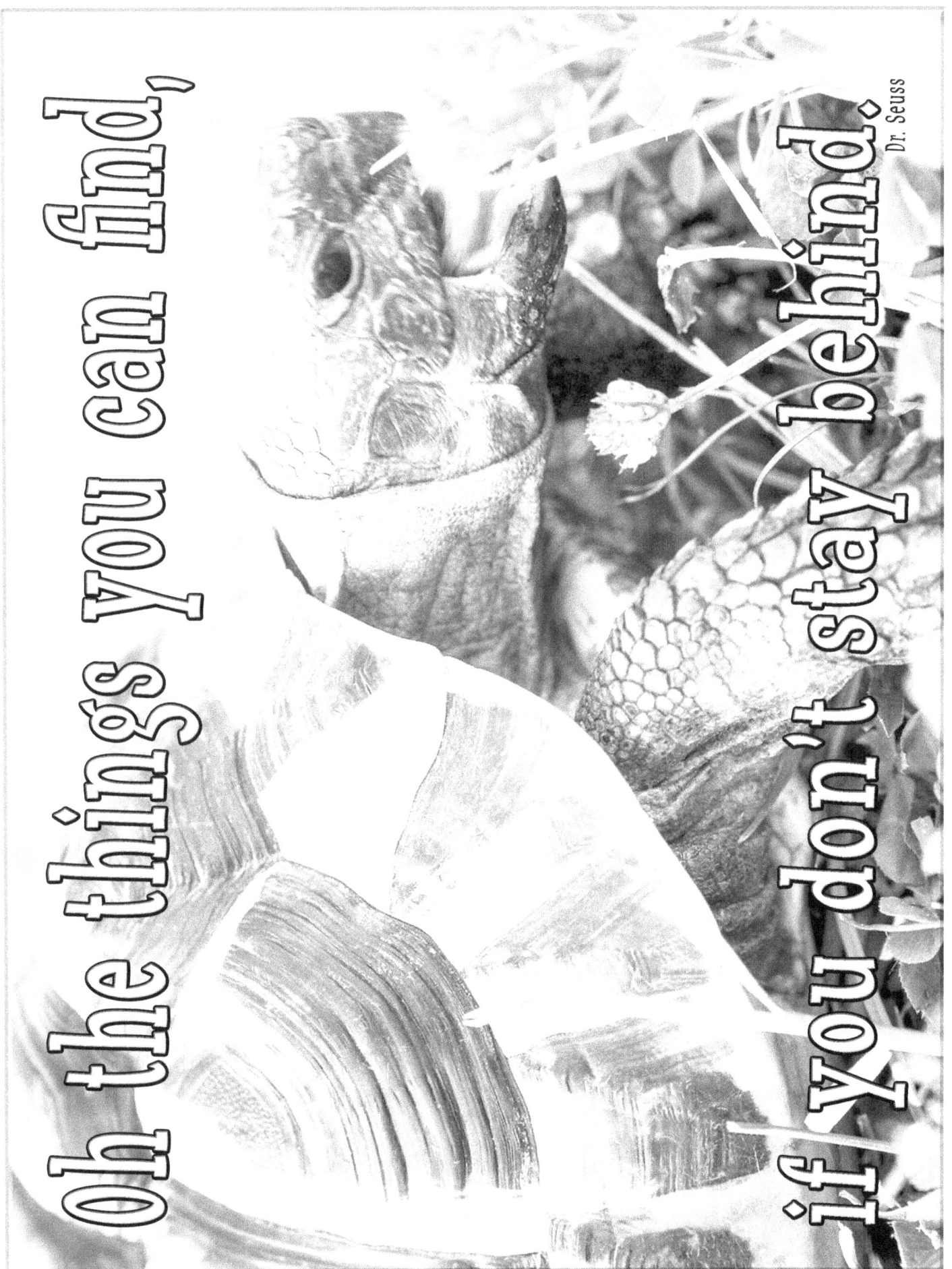

Yesterday you said tomorrow. Just do it. —Nike

Adult Coloring Book
Baby Animals

In this inspiring grayscale coloring book, I have included thirty original and delightful illustrations of adorable baby animals to motivate your imagination and inspire your inner-artist. In grayscale coloring, you work blending colors together following the shading of the image to guide you. Each drawing comes with an inspisational quote by a famous person and invites you to experiment and play with colors, letting them relax your mind and relieve your stress. If you like this book, please take a moment to post a review on www.amazon.com

Enjoy.

Samantha Moore

About Samantha Moore

Since childhood artist Samantha Moore has been experimenting with colors and their influence on mood and relaxation. She has a degree in Graphic Design, a diploma in Art History and is a Reiki certified therapist.

Copyright © 2020 L. Romo. All rights reserved. With the exception of photocopying for personal use and book review, no part of this book may be reproduced in any form without the written permission of the copyright owner.

Adult Coloring Book Baby Animals

ISBN: **9798602971439**

Please feel free to contact us if you have any questions or comments: whatacolourfulworld@mail.com

You may also like:

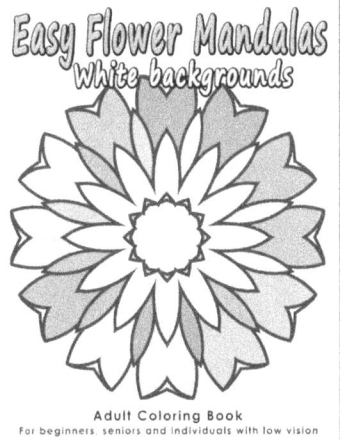 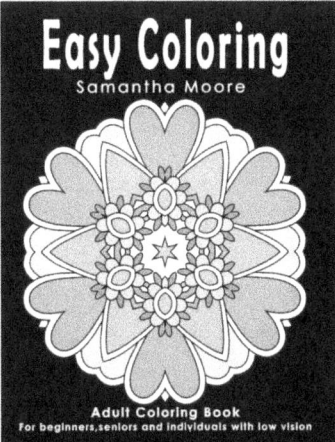 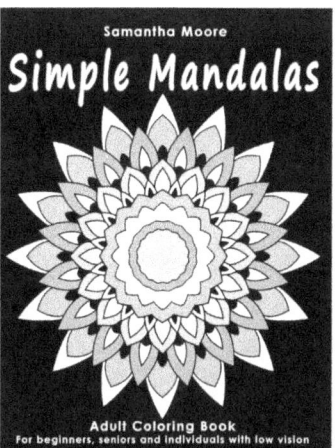

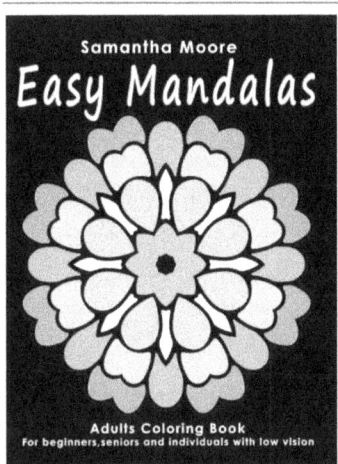 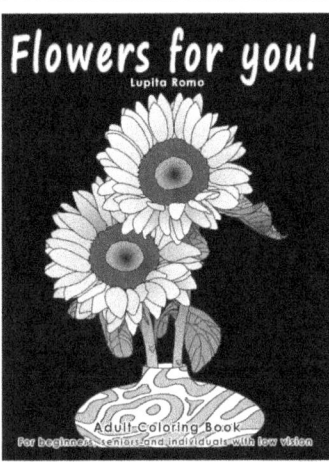 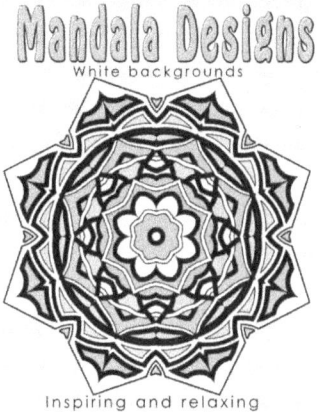

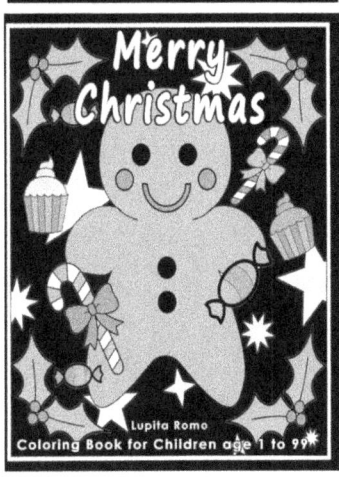 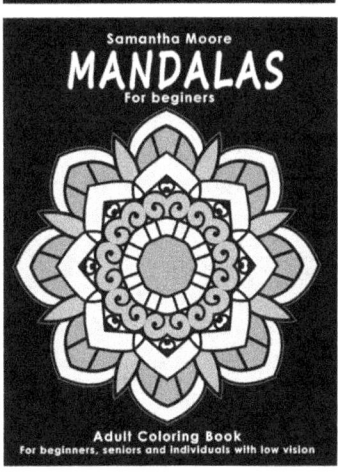 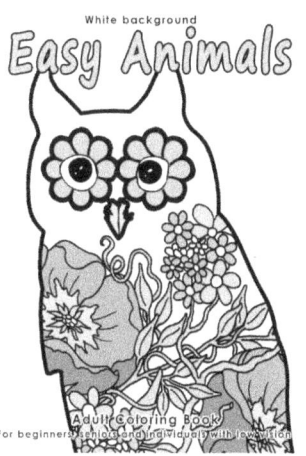

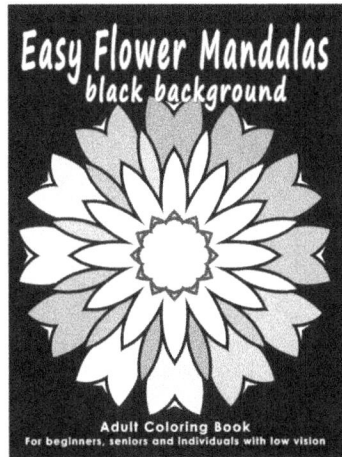
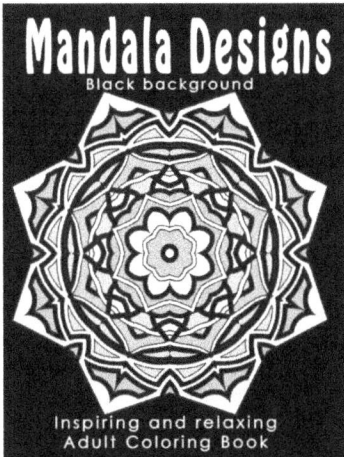
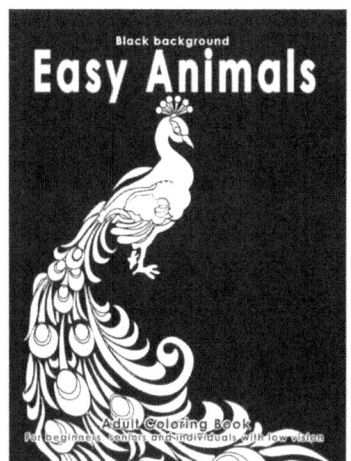
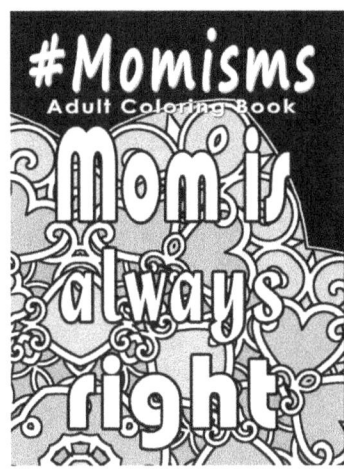
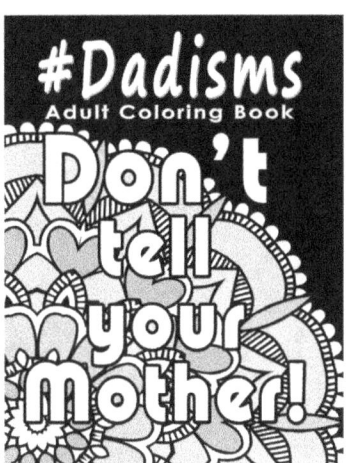

We would love to receive your comments. Please, find a moment to write a review.

Thank you.

www.ingramcontent.com/pod-product-compliance
Lightning Source LLC
Chambersburg PA
CBHW080525220526
45465CB00006B/2607